Succule
in the Garden

Attila Kapitany and Rudolf Schulz

SP

Sempervivum flowers

Reprint 2007 Attila Kapitany and Rudolf Schulz

All rights reserved. No part of this book may be reproduced in any form or by any means without prior permission in writing from both authors.

ISBN 0 9585167 4 X

Schulz Publishing
3 Norwhich St,.Boronia, VIC 3155, Australia
tarrex@ozemail.com.au
gecko@connexus.net.au

Printed by Everbest Printing Co Ltd, China

Acknowledgements

We thank:
Victor and Christina Aprozeanu, Shirley-Anne Bell, Fiona Brockhoff, Les and Honey Denyer, Suzie Forge, Brian Gerrard, Jim and Julie Hall, Alexander Harris, Paul Klaassen, Michele Mackay, William Martin and Diana Morgan.

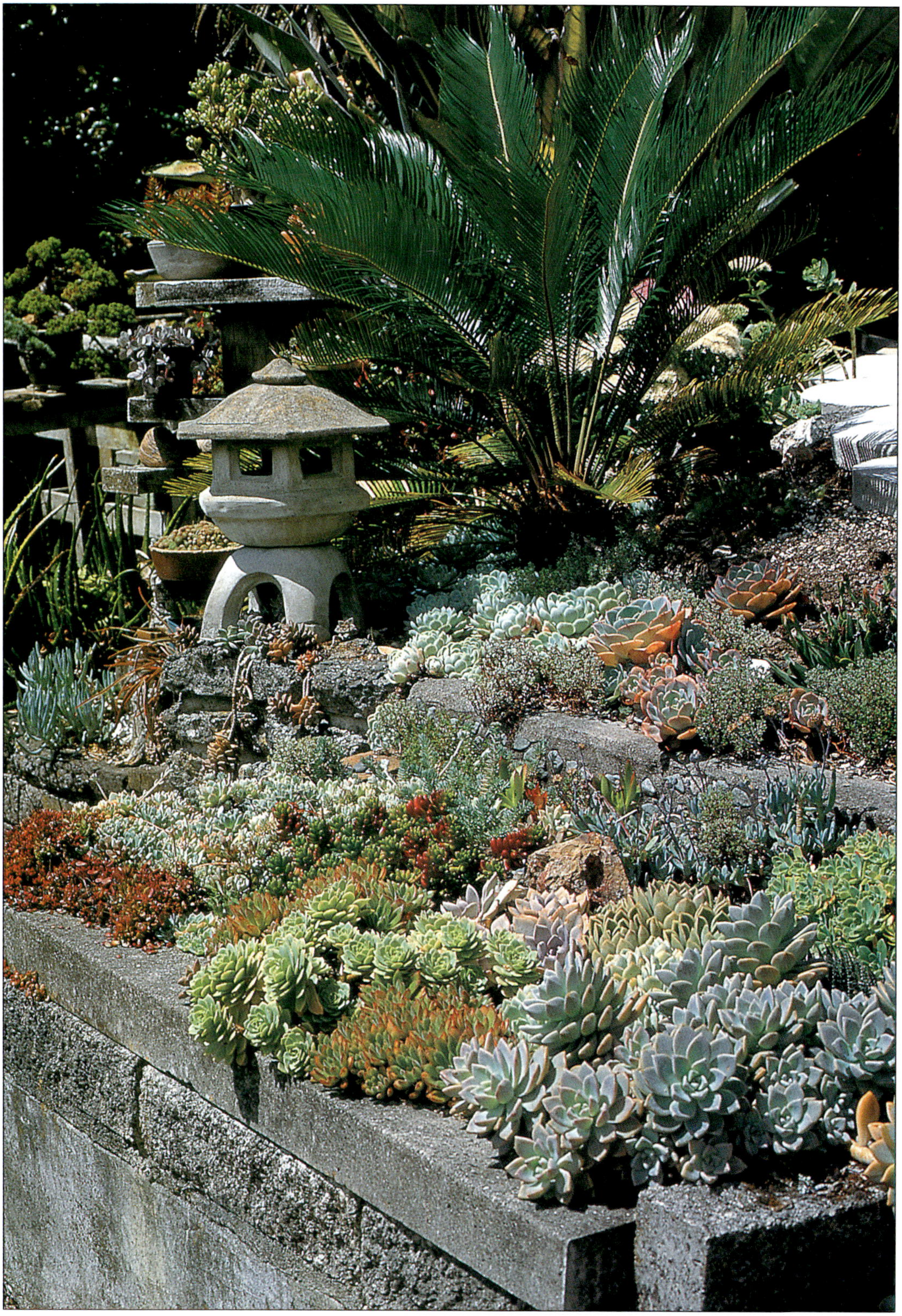

Contents

Introduction 6

The best expert advice cannot match common sense and local knowledge in determining which plants will be successful for you in your garden.

Nature's garden 14

Views from around the world of succulents growing under adverse conditions in their natural habitat. Analysis of how habitat conditions can be used to grow better succulents in our gardens.

City courtyard 22

A busy lifestyle, high walls and confined spaces without much room and time to garden still allow for smaller potted combinations that can be enjoyed year round. Beautifully grown and presented rosettes of echeverias are a major focus.

Suburban nature strip 32

A small compact nature strip garden as an alternative to a lawn. This garden features many cold-loving and alpine succulents. Well over a hundred different types of succulents are crowded beautifully into a very small area.

50 Seaside garden

Gardening poses its own special challenges by the sea, with often windy and very salty conditions. This succulent garden blends aesthetically with the natural environment, which is mostly indigenous seaside flora.

60 Country farmlet

A waterwise and practical garden in a lightly forested rural area. Succulent bottle trees dominate and provide shade around the farm dam. Aside from the decorative uses of succulents, some practical aspects are also examined.

78 Hillside country garden

A dry hillside of gravel has been transformed into a lavish garden blending many differing plant types, of which succulents have come to play an important part. A garden of tasteful harmonies and contrasts.

92 Arid inland garden

Very hot and dry open spaces can be difficult, and yet here a transformation into a cactus garden on a grand scale was created.

104 Index

Introduction

Will these plants grow for me in my garden or house? How big will they grow and will they flower? These common questions are asked at one time or another by every gardener. With succulents the answer is simple. They can and will grow and flower for anybody, but not everywhere. What makes for successful succulent gardening is experimentation, one key to success. It is not uncommon to have gardeners trial plants in their garden for their suitability, at times just moving them from place to place to determine the best results. Garden conditions in this book may be similar to your own and help as a guide in determining what plants will most likely succeed in your garden.

Worldwide, where frosts are not too severe or regular, many species of succulents can be grown in the garden. Places include Australia, New Zealand, South Africa and the southern areas of the USA and Europe. Gardeners worldwide have always been trying to grow plants that may not exactly suit their climate. They are challenged by trying and testing plants to their limits. Those who persevere with experimentation will quickly find their way with succulents. Though many are very hardy and easy, there are just as many that can be difficult and very challenging. A book on how to grow succulents which gives detailed growing information about each plant would require far too numerous regional versions to suit all the different geographical regions of the world. We would rather, as with this book, explore some of the wonderful examples of successful succulent gardening, based on experimentation and common sense gardening techniques. Other literature on how to grow cactus and succulents is easy to find, just visit any public library. Closer inspection and comparison of several of these books may expose contradictions, because each author is biased by his or her personal knowledge and experience which will often be limited to only one country.

Simple answers often do not work. For example, we might recommend that a plant needs a sunny window sill as with lithops ('living stones'). One person's sunny window sill may be totally different to another. How many hours of sun does the window sill get? Two hours, three or maybe more? Is it morning

Success can be as simple as choosing the right plant for the right spot. This *Echeveria 'Afterglow'* is unattended and growing well in full sun.

sun, midday or late afternoon? Midday sun which exceeds two hours can even kill lithops. If lithops are in small black plastic pots (which will absorb more heat than other coloured pots), the midday sun as well as the afternoon sun can be harmful. Are there any trees or greenery outside the window that may shade or soften the incoming light and heat? The size of the window and window edging, the presence of curtains, the type of glass, and ventilation can make the difference between success and failure. Common sense and an awareness of your own unique growing conditions are much more important than the information on a plant tag or a nurseryperson's advice.

So what about the garden? Do any of the same complex problems exist here? They do, though the garden is a more natural environment for any plant than indoor situations, making it far easier to be successful. It would be fair to say that all plants will do better outdoors than indoors. Where over 80% of all indoor plants purchased will most likely have died within 12 months, over 80% of all garden plants purchased will probably have survived, often having improved in appearance and size. Some succulents have the highest survival rates of any plants whether kept indoors or out.

Aside from experimentation, there are many ways by which people seek to learn about succulents and their care. Often they visit their local nursery or garden centre for plants and advice. Many people who have ventured down this path have found it well short of their expectations. The range of plants available in many garden centres is

Where and how people use succulents can be very imaginative, often going beyond what most gardening books recommend. Here a mixture of smaller rosette succulents fills the spacings between concrete steps.

Used in modern garden design, the common, old-fashioned *Echeveria imbricata* is given a new lease of life when planted imaginatively with other plants. Above is a large *Aloe arborescens* embracing two rosettes of *Echeveria imbricata*. Another use for *E. imbricata* is shown on the opposite page.

often poor and just as often what is available may not be in the very best of health, and advice, while appreciated, is often lacking in experience or depth of knowledge.

Another common method used to learn about succulents is to buy or borrow a book as a reference work for guidance on names and varieties. Use any cultural advice within all books cautiously! In which country was the book written? Are the conditions for growing them the same as in your country? Are the plants listed in the book available in your area? Often succulent books, with all good intentions, list many plants that are very new, hard to obtain, or rare. As you turn the pages and see something that catches your eye and imagination, you may want one. Often photographs of plants do not have a scale that lets the reader know how big it is or how it grows. Many succulent lovers have fallen prey to photographs of attractive plants only to be disappointed later.

We recommend that gardeners take a walk down streets in their area, look into gardens and see what does and does not grow well. It will not take long before you find succulents of some sort, especially in established suburbs. If it is a nice day, you may well be lucky to catch a gardener in his or her version of paradise. Don't be shy! Gardeners are often good talkers who love to chat (and boast!) about their plants. The local knowledge from such gardeners will be invaluable in saving you a lot of trial and error. Another good way of gaining insight into succulents and their culture is to visit or join a local garden club. Most city councils will be able to help you locate one. Internet listings of clubs and societies in your area can also be tried. Garden clubs and societies are very helpful, even if you do not join but go along to a few meetings with a list of questions. Someone there will have most of the answers or at least know of a gardener who does. They can recommend locally hardy types of succulents and the location of the nearest reputable succulent supplier. Members often bring along spare cuttings to sell or give away. After one or two visits to a meeting you may even want to join up for a year's membership.

Who would have thought succulents and annuals could mix well in the garden? With experimentation anything is possible. Here *Echeveria imbricata* grows happily amongst annual alyssums.

The best way of all to enjoy and access succulents, as well as good reliable information about them, is to track down a succulent society. They are not hard to find, and if there is not one where you live, you can still do as many members have and correspond by mail or e-mail. Succulent society members are a treasure trove of information and love to share their interest with like-minded people. If a plant is in a book, and it is available, society members will know where to get it. Succulent society meetings usually have plants for sale at very reasonable prices and also have very good libraries.

Successful growers seem to have a personal relationship with their plants. They read their plants almost like a book by noting the slight changes that succulents exhibit. In early spring shrunken plant bodies begin to swell and sprout shoots. In response to these signs, a good gardener may fertilise and provide extra water. These succulents usually reward the care giver with good growth and flowers. To feel the soil for dryness, to observe the weather and be vigilant for pests and diseases is not a chore for gardeners who enjoy gardening.

Each and every garden will reflect its own unique limitations as well as opportunities and challenges. In the following chapters, we will look at gardeners who have seen the opportunities and met the challenges. Each of their gardens is very different from the next. This reflects two main points, the individuality of the creative gardener and the garden's unique conditions. While some gardens in this book are on a grand scale covering several acres, others are smaller and one is a diminutive courtyard.

The larger the garden available, the larger the plants that can be grown. It also allows for faster and larger growing varieties to be used. The gardeners who have less room, being closer to a large city, have focused more on the smaller decorative rosette succulents such as echeverias and sedums. It is interesting to note that these smaller gardens are all very tactile in nature and hence people friendly. The larger country gardens seem to have spinier, more dangerous looking types of succulents.

The variety of gardens chosen for this book reflect the garden types that are commonly found in many parts of the world: seaside, suburban, inner city courtyard, small farm, country hillside and hot dry country. What each of these gardeners can grow well in their unique situation may not grow as well in, or suit, one of the others.

What happens when an old garden is abandoned? While most plants perish, some succulents seem to last forever. These *Aloe ferox* still grace the front of this now empty house.

While some succulent types can be found in several gardens, most of the gardeners have gathered their own selection of preferred plants which works well for them. A great deal of useful information and many interesting ideas can be drawn from looking closely at how and why these gardens are created and maintained. You will find ideas for problem areas in the garden such as dry areas, under trees, salty and sandy soil, windy areas, bushfire prone areas, small gardens, shallow soil, steep slopes and bare embankments.

It is one thing for us to talk about all the great virtues of using succulents in the gardens as we have done in our first two books, and another thing altogether to present real life situations as we have done in this book. The gardens in this book are all private gardens, created by the toil of the owners themselves. No caretaker or landscaper consulted, used or needed. Common sense and practicality led these gardeners to develop an interest in succulents.

So why are all these gardeners now so excited about succulents? Because they 'work'. It can be as simple as that.

Sedum morganianum in a hanging basket. Even the experts and their books do not always know how a plant will grow. *S. morganianum* is said to grow to 1 m in length and yet here the stems are well over twice that length.

Climate extremes

Gardeners have always been challenging plants to perform in their unique climates, at times with extremes that really test both plant and gardener. Here we look at two examples. One is the wet tropics, the other a very cold and wet climate. It is common practice in colder and wetter parts of the world for gardeners to be vigilant when plants are small, covering them from the cold. This is more important in the first year of establishment in the garden. The closer to the ground, the more severe the frost damage will be. As plants increase in size and age they naturally increase their ability to survive without extra care. Where cold climate conditions are harsher still, sensitive succulents, as with some bulbs, are lifted from the ground in autumn and stored in dry places like a shed until spring.

◄◄ Singapore Botanical Gardens has a sun rockery in which many succulents can be found growing well. The tropical heat, humidity and rainfall pose their own special problems. Prior to seeing this for ourselves, we would not have recommended growing succulents in the wet tropics.

▲ Yuccas, agaves and sun hardy bromeliads such as *Annanus comosum variegatum* blend well together in the Singapore Botanical Gardens. To the right is a large *Euphorbia lactea* with some *Gasteria* species underneath its dense canopy. To the left and centre front is *Yucca aloifolia*. In the background right is *Agave angustifolia variegata*.

◄ A raised garden bed of mixed sempervivum species with a central planting of *Aloe aristata*.

►► England has very cold winters with short daylight hours, frequent rain and even snow. This is the same planting as in the above picture; now snow covered after a mid-winter snowstorm.

▼ *Agave americana* under snow cover. Only extremely wet and boggy conditions seem to trouble these tough plants.
(Photos on this page by Neville Bell from Glenhurst Cactus Nursery, UK.)

INTRODUCTION 13

Succulents in their natural environment

Aside from Antarctica, succulent plants are found on all continents. The driest continent, Australia, has surprisingly few native succulents, largely because of its history of prolonged droughts. At first this seems illogical since succulents have an adaptation to dry periods. They do, but only to short, predictable dry seasons, not the prolonged dry spells characteristic of parts of inland Australia.

The continent with the greatest number of succulents is Africa. Again, we see almost no succulents in the driest area, the Sahara desert, while the southernmost west coast of South Africa has the greatest number of species. This area has mild dry summers but experiences a definite and regular wet season every year. The eastern areas of South Africa also have many succulents and these experience the opposite and more common climate conditions, having a dry winter and a wetter summer. The cactus family of succulents from the Americas are also mostly from areas with regular summer wet seasons. However, there are some exceptions to this generalisation.

The true deserts of the world are mostly barren, even of succulents. Semi-deserts however, are not as arid and may have regular, yearly rain patterns, and often have regular flooding for short periods.

⏷ Gardens with succulents have often been designed to represent a stylized version of their natural habitat. This gives the impression to those who are not familiar with succulents in habitat that they grow as thickly and lushly as seen here. What gardens like this prove is that most succulents will still grow in a humid and wet climate very unlike their own natural environment.

Succulents abound here because it is still too dry for forests or grasslands to exist, both of which offer too much competition to succulents for light and space.

Succulents that come from areas with wet climates grow in special dry environments within forests, on cliffs, on rock outcrops or in areas of very infertile soil where other plants have a difficult time thriving. Such areas range from the European Alps to cold, wind-swept Patagonia as well as the steaming tropics of South America, Africa and Asia. This diversity of habitat and environment makes it difficult to make sweeping generalizations on succulent care.

After visiting many habitats where succulents grow naturally, we found that within the natural range of succulents the poorest surviving specimens are often in the hottest and driest locations, whereas the more attractive and healthier specimens appear to grow in places where more water and better soil are available.

Do not try to grow succulents in the same way as you assume that they survive in nature. It is almost impossible to replicate their environment and not desirable for the plants. Understanding their native climate and environment does however have some benefits. Most important is to know when succulents have their growing season and when they are dormant (whether they are winter or summer growers). Some succulents require a definite rest from being watered during their dormant period but most species are not so fussy and will adjust to the regular growing patterns of other plants in the garden, resting in winter or the colder months, and growing in the warmer months. Also to be learnt from habitat is whether succulents come from hot or cold climates, very dry or wetter climates, experience frosts or are tropical and can be grown year round.

▲ Natural gardens seldom look as stereotypical as this view taken in the Atacama desert of Chile. This hyper-arid desert is 99% devoid of life with only a narrow coastal strip supporting sparse vegetation. This photograph was taken in one of the most 'lush' oases!

▼ After rain in the Atacama desert, succulent *Calandrinia* species quickly germinate. This plant is actual size.

Paul Klaassan

16 SUCCULENTS IN HABITAT

▲ Mists rolling in from the Pacific Ocean provide enough moisture to allow succulents to survive on the coastal edge of the Atacama Desert in Chile.

▼ This stark, almost totally biologically empty section of the Namib desert is home to the strange looking *Welwitchia mirabilis*. This plant is not a succulent, instead it obtains its water from very deep down in the gravelly soils. With very few exceptions, succulents find all desert habitats too hot and dry.

◀ *Aloe pillansii*, growing on a low hill south of the Orange River in coastal South Africa. While the low valleys are almost devoid of life, the hilltops receive just enough mist and fog to support succulent growth. These ancient and now deteriorating giants are the remains of a once extensive 'forest' which grew in this desert when it had a wetter enviroment.

▶ A typical habitat for succulents which is characterized by a covering of low sparse shrubs. Note how the cactus (and also various succulent species) grow in the shelter of the shrubs. Here they receive some shade and also benefit from any light rain which runs down the stems of the shrubs.

SUCCULENTS IN HABITAT 17

◄◄ *Aloe khamiesensis* growing in the western Cape Province of South Africa. This species grows mostly on rocky outcrops. This is because the flat areas seen behind the aloes are covered by a dense shrub cover which is prone to wildfires. Damaging winter frosts also are quite severe on the flatter slopes. This area of South Africa is home to over 1000 species of succulent plants but they are not uniformly scattered over the countryside. Instead, the great majority are clustered in favourable habitats such as rocky slopes and southwest facing hillsides (where they are more exposed to the prevailing coastal mists).

▼ High mountains are not initially thought of as places where succulents thrive. In drier regions, such as here in inland Peru, the rainfall is extremely low and competition from other plants is also low. These factors have allowed some succulents, such as the giant *Puya raimondii*, pictured here, to thrive and grow to huge proportions. The flower spikes are over 6 m tall! The altitude of this site is over 5000 m and almost every night of the year there is a frost.

▶▶ Rainforests can also have dry places. Located in southern Brazil, this north facing cliff face is home to a wide assortment of succulents which find the abundant sunlight, air movement, good drainage, regular waterings and lack of competition ideal. If all of these conditions can be replicated in our gardens, the result will be rapid, healthy growth.

◀ *Agave bracteosa* growing on a cliff face in Mexico. This thornless species normally grows in soil but will access any surface which provides it with enough nutrients, support and water. The advantage of growing here is obvious—no competition!

▼ Rocky environments in moist habitats are often very rich in succulent species. Here, an *Echeveria* species grows on a mossy and lichen encrusted rock face in Peru. Normally, mosses and succulents are not thought of as sharing the same environment but in this case they both benefit from shade and a mostly damp environment. The related sedums and sempervivums (also in the *Crassula* family) all come from windy, mountainous and often cool climates.

◀◀ Succulents grow well when supplied with abundant water. In the hills above Marathon, Texas, an *Agave harvardiana* is growing right alongside a seasonal seepage. Note how the lush background vegetation indicates that this a relatively moist environment during the summer rainy season. During the dry season, the shrubs and small trees become deciduous but this agave will continue to look spectacular.

▼ A very unlikely habitat for succulents? Not at all! Even the area around Iguacu Falls on the Brazil-Argentina border supports more species of succulents than most true desert environments. The rocky outcrops on the left are home to a number of species which thrive in the windy but moist waterfall environment. For a short period during the dry season the falls reduce in volume and this rocky environment becomes too dry for other plants, allowing succulents to dominate in what would otherwise be a rainforest habitat.

▶ With rice growing in the valley, this Madagascar habitat is anything but dry. Rocky outcrops, however, dry very quickly even during rainy periods. The bare rocks in the foreground have just enough soil in their cracks to support *Euphorbia milii* ('crown of thorns'). The bare areas in the background are home to at least nine other succulent species including aloes, kalanchoes and pachypodiums.

▼ *Trichocereus pasacana* growing in a seasonal watercourse in Argentina. These giants of the cactus world are over 10 m tall. They thrive best on the relatively moist but well draining gravelly soil in the valley. Note how the drier hillsides are devoid of this species.

A side bench with the best-looking succulents on show. Plants are rotated regularly for a change of scene.

A city courtyard

Diana gardens within the confines of high walls that surround her inner city property. Space is at a premium and yet a great deal is achieved within the small area. Diana loves flowers in the house and for over thirty years she has gardened with everything from annuals, bulbs and 'old world' roses. These are still grown around the narrow side and back garden of the house. Having a naturally busy lifestyle and raising four children, less time was spent in the garden than she would have liked. Succulents with their year round beauty and ease of care, proved themselves an ideal element in this garden. A flow of garden interest from one thing to another led her to an appreciation of practical, common sense succulents, which now came to the fore as the right plants for the right spot. It is here in the courtyard, which separates the house from the front gate, where Diana tends her most favoured succulents, the echeverias.

▲ From the front door the view across the courtyard is enjoyed.

▼ When not in use, a small outdoor coffee table is used to display imaginative plantings.

A CITY COURTYARD 23

Arranging and mixing pots

All the succulents are in pots of various types and sizes. Diana finds that the type of pot makes all the difference to how the plant looks. Of course, there is the added bonus of being able to move the potted plants into arrangements that would otherwise not be possible if planted in the garden.

◀◀ Bringing the best plant forward can be enjoyable, especially when visitors come over.

▼ A large decorative concrete pot, mass planted with *Graptopetalum paraguayense* and *Sedum nussbaumerianum*, (brownish-golden leaves). This pot was planted up four years ago.

▸▸ Choosing the right shapes and colours of pots to suit individual plants is half the fun.

◂◂ Three ceramic pots, tiered by height. To the right is *Echeveria* 'Afterglow'. In the foreground is *E. lilacina*. To the left is *E.* 'Rococo'.

▾ Textures and colours are not restricted to the plants alone. From left to right are *Echeveria* 'Bittersweet' and *E.* 'Fireball' with an unnamed hybrid in the foreground.

A CITY COURTYARD 25

Echeverias on show

Diana has refined her pleasure with succulents over time to the point where the genus *Echeveria* now dominates her choice of plants. This is partly due to their neat flower like leaf arrangements, which go well with her floral interests elsewhere. While echeverias prevail, the courtyard also contains sempervivums, aeoniums, kalanchoes and aloes, all of which provide additional texture and leaf forms.

▲ *Echeveria 'Fasciculata'*

▼ *Echeveria 'Bittersweet'*

▼ There is no shortage of flowers or colour from these echeverias. On the left is *Echeveria multicaulis*. The large leaves of *Echeveria 'Bittersweet'* are on the right.

26 A CITY COURTYARD

Echeveria elegans

Echeveria 'Topsy Turvy'

Echeveria pallida

Echeveria 'Lucita'

Echeveria 'Arlie Wright'

Echeveria 'Big Red'

Echeveria 'Mauna Loa'

Echeveria 'Red Edge'

Having fun

Fantasies can be created with plants. It all started with Diana's daughter, then aged two, who would help plant a large bowl garden with stones and a few common succulents. They were small and tactile and could be used like living building blocks. Together, they made a little hill and some paths and created stories as they played.

▼ This 300 mm long bonsai dish planted with a mixture of succulents in early spring took only three months to fill out. Once crowded together, they grow a great deal slower.

▼ The imagination runs wild with some of the plantings. *Graptoveria* 'Huth's Pink' is growing out of the pot walls.

▼ *Sempervivum tectorum* looking natural on this old tree root.

▶▶ An old echeveria stem has had its head cut off. The stem has been put around the side of the house, where it will offset.

▼ Bulbs and succulents growing together. For three years miniature daffodils have come up in this bowl with *Echeveria 'Violet Queen'*. After flowering, the untidy drooping leaves are tied into knots to keep the bowl looking neat and yet still interesting.

A CITY COURTYARD 29

Further information on plants illustrated or grown in this garden

Plants	main attraction	flower colour	usage	shade tolerance	pot suitability
Aloe plicatilis (not pictured)	foliage	orange/red	sculpture	low	excellent
Echeveria 'Afterglow' photo page 25	leaf colour	pink/orange	rosette	low	excellent
Echeveria 'Arlie Wright' photo page 27	foliage	pink/orange	rosette	low	excellent
Echeveria 'Big Red' photo page 27	symmetry leaf colour	pink/orange	rosette	low	excellent
Echeveria 'Bitter Sweet' photo page 26	foliage	orange/pink	rosette	low	excellent
Echeveria 'Blue Curl' photo page 27	leaf colour symmetry	orange/pink	rosette	low	excellent
Echeveria derenbergii (not pictured)	symmetry	red/yellow	rosette	low	excellent
Echeveria 'Doris Taylor' (not pictured)	foliage flowers	orange/yellow	en masse rosette	moderate	yes
Echeveria elegans photo page 27	foliage symmetry	pink	en masse	low	excellent
Echeveria 'Fasciculata' photo page 26	foliage	pink/orange	sculpture	low	excellent
Echeveria lilacina photo page 25	leaf colour symmetry	pink/orange	rosette	low	excellent
Echeveria 'Mauna Loa' photo page 27	foliage	pink/orange	sculpture	low	excellent
Echeveria pallida photo page 27	foliage	green/pink	sculpture	low	yes
Echeveria 'Red Edge' photo page 27	leaf colour symmetry	pink/orange	en masse rosette	low	excellent
Echeveria 'Rococo' photo page 25	foliage	pink/orange	rosette	low	excellent
Echeveria 'Topsy Turvy' photo page 27	shape leaf colour	orange	en masse rosette	low	yes
Echeveria 'Violet Queen' photo page 29	foliage leaf colour	pink	en masse rosette	moderate	excellent
Graptopetalum paraguayense photo page 24	symmetry leaf colour	cream	en masse rosette	low	yes
Sedum nussbaumerianum photo page 24	leaf colour	white	en masse	low	yes
Sempervivum tectorum photo page 28	symmetry leaf colour	green/pink	en masse rosette	moderate	yes

*Height and width are based on favorable garden situations and beginning with an 80 mm size pot plant.

suitability for indoor situations	height & width after 1 year*	height & width after 5 years*	how does it spread?	usual method of propagation	additional information
sunny position	0.2 x 0.2 m	1 m x 1m	solitary	cuttings	frost hardy
sunny position	0.1 x 0.1 m	0.2 x 0.3 m	mostly solitary	head cuts	colour best in winter
sunny position	0.1 x 0.2 m	0.3 x 0.2 m	mostly solitary	head cuts	prune heads
sunny position	0.1 x 0.2 m	0.2 x 0.3 m	mostly solitary	head cuts	prune heads
sunny position	0.1 x 0.2 m	0.2 x 0.3 m	mostly solitary	head cuts	prune heads
sunny position	0.1 x 0.5 m	0.2 x 0.3 m	mostly solitary	few offsets head cuts	prune heads
sunny position	0.1 x 0.1 m	0.1 x 0.2 m	offsets	offsets	miniature
not recommended	0.1 x 0.1 m	0.2 x 0.2 m	offsets	offsets	frost hardy
not recommended	0.1 x 0.1 m	0.1 x 0.3 m	offsets	offsets	frost hardy
not recommended	0.1 x 0.1 m	0.2 x 0.3 m	mostly solitary	head cuts	prune heads
sunny position	0.1 x 0.1 m	0.1 x 0.2 m	mostly solitary	leaves	needs good ventilation
not recommended	0.2 x 0.3 m	0.5 x 0.4 m	mostly solitary	head cuts	prune heads
not recommended	0.1 x 0.2m	0.4 x 0.3 m	mostly solitary	head cuts	prune heads
not recommended	0.1 x 0.1 m	0.2 x 0.2 m	offsets	offsets	frost hardy colour best in winter
sunny position	0.1 x 0.1 m	0.1x 0.2 m	mostly solitary	head cuts	tolerates light frost
not recommended	0.1 x 0.1 m	0.1 x 0.2 m	offsets	offsets	stress improves shape
not recommended	0.1 x 0.2 m	0.1 x 0.2 m	offsets	offsets	colours best in autumn frost hardy
sunny position	0.1 x 0.1 m	0.2 x 0.4 m	sprawling	cuttings	prune for shape
not recommended	0. 1 x 0.1 m	0.2 x 0.4 m	sprawling	cuttings	prune to keep tidy stress improves colour
not recommended	0.1 x 0.1 m	0.1 x 0.2 m	offsets	offsets	frost hardy

A nature strip

Michele lives on an average size quarter acre suburban block with an established garden full of mature trees with a thick and shaded understory. Her pleasure in gardening covers all plant types and this can be seen by the seemingly overcrowded and mixed 'forest', as she calls it. Several years ago Michele decided to expand her garden on to the roadside nature strip and now this small area contains over 100 species of succulents. As this grass covered area was mostly sunny and dry with poor soil, she knew that whatever was chosen would probably have a hard time and for the most part be neglected. The nature strip was the last place left with any lawn, and as this was the garden type that demanded the most work, it was an easy decision to replace it with succulents. Over the following years and with some experimentation, she found that her new succulent garden had become her pride and joy, full of surprises year round. Initially, she thought that succulents in a garden would present themselves as fairly static. To her surprise and great pleasure she discovered that there were dramatic changes from month to month, as well as from season to season. She inspects the area regularly just for pleasure and always finds enjoyable things to do because the plants are always changing.

In this chapter we will explore some of the seasonal highlights and changes that are not obvious to those who have not gardened with succulents for a long period. Also featured in this chapter are some sedums and sempervivums which have traditionally been considered alpine plants.

A nature strip, looking its best and greenest. In the cooler months of the year this lawn area required the most work of all in the garden. During the warmer months it dried out and often had yellow and brown patches.

▶ Michele stands outside her property, which contains many tall trees and shrubs. A dry summer looms, as lawns begin to show signs of dying.

▼ Other than the well known *Sedum 'Autumn Joy'*, little reliable information exists on the flowering performance of most other succulents.

▼ Preparation: set the family a task! First a lawn killer was used and then the soil and clay was loosened. Additional gravel and soil was added for better drainage.

A NATURE STRIP 33

Foliage plants.

The first planting of succulents in this nature strip garden were small in size. Within twelve months most individuals had multiplied and spread. Many of the first plants were chosen for their foliage not their flowers.

▼ This garden was originally planted to provide year-round foliage colour

▲ Dramatic leaf colour combinations that change with the seasons add interest to this garden.

▶ *Echeveria 'Violet Queen'*, showing summer colours, has multiplied from one plant into several in one season's growth.

◀ *Graptoveria 'Huth's Pink'* in its winter flush.

▲ *Echeveria 'Violet Queen'* with winter colours. Cold and frosty weather brings out the best in this plant.

▼ *Aeonium 'Zwartkop'*. With leaves like this, who needs flowers?

A NATURE STRIP 35

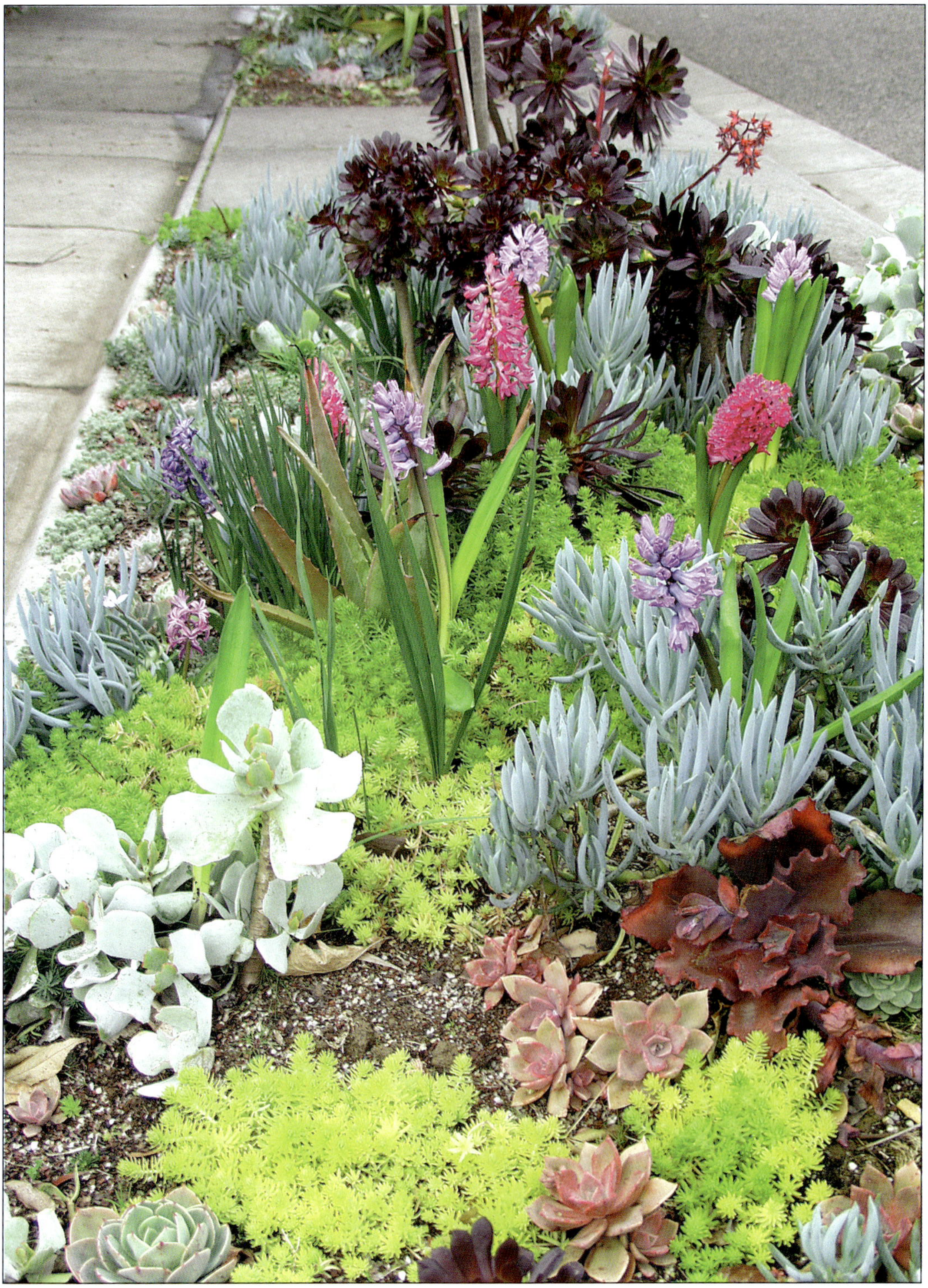

Spring bulbs

One year a friend gave Michele some dry, unwanted and unnamed bulbs. Not having the heart to throw them out they were planted in a very sunny part of the succulent garden and forgotten. To her surprise, they all came up in the following spring and bloomed beautifully. Since then more have been planted to complement the whole planting. One of the reasons that most spring bulbs do well in this garden is that they have deep roots that grow straight down, while succulents generally have very shallow roots. As a result, they can co-exist harmoniously.

◥ Hyacinths and jonquils with *Senecio mandraliscae* in the foreground.

◢ These were the very first flowers which revealed the location of the forgotten bulbs. Two green *Sedum mexicanum* varieties and the blue *Senecio mandralisca* surround a pink hyacinth and a 'star flower' (*Triteleia* sp.)

◣ A jonquil flowering against a backdrop of blue *Senecio mandraliscae* makes for good contrast.

Annual succulents

As the early spring bulbs finish their flowering cycle the self-sown annual succulent, *Dorotheanthus bellidoniformis* rises to take the stage. Several years ago Michele planted some seedlings, and since then they have been coming up naturally each year. Originally they were to fill out bare patches between larger or slower growing succulents. As they were so successful, they are now welcome and encouraged wherever there is space for them.

Portulaca grandiflora is another well known annual succulent which is being used during the summer months in much the same way as the *Dorotheanthus* is used during spring.

▲ *Dorotheanthus bellidoniformis* (Livingstone daisies) carpeting the ground with colour.

▼ Some of the many colours of Livingston daisies.

▼ Livingstone daisies shimmering in the afternoon sun. At different times in the day and in different lighting conditions they seem to change their colouration.

▼ In lightly shaded places Livingstone daisies can still flower well, but with a deeper glowing colour. As each flower opens for the first time, it is more intense, with some yellow colouring, which fades to white after a few days.

▲ Glistening like ice crystals, special water storage cells add another dimension to *Dorotheanthus bellidoniformis*.

▲ During the peak of a long, dry summer, these succulents appear to be faring well. All the patches of bright colour are *Portulaca grandiflora*.

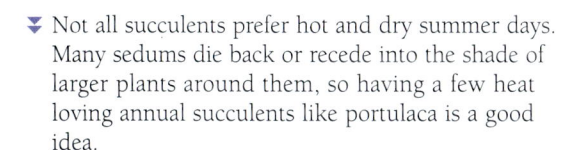

▼ *Portulaca* hybrids showing vivid summer colours.

▼ Not all succulents prefer hot and dry summer days. Many sedums die back or recede into the shade of larger plants around them, so having a few heat loving annual succulents like portulaca is a good idea.

A NATURE STRIP

Sedums

It may be hard to imagine where there could be enough room for so many different plant types in this small garden, especially during late summer, when the annual dorotheanthus finishes flowering. From beneath and among them, sedums quickly rise like an explosion, as if it is their time for sun and glory. Sedums come in many shapes and forms, however Michele has chosen to use hardy, fast-growing ground cover varieties only. These are generally miniatures that carpet the ground wherever they are used. Primarily grown for their foliage, their regular seasonal flowers come as an added bonus. Through winter and early spring, sedums are mostly withdrawn and compact in growth. From mid to late spring they stretch out, increasing their volume by up to five times before flowering.

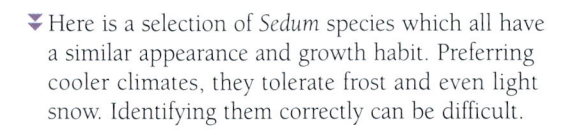

▼ Here is a selection of *Sedum* species which all have a similar appearance and growth habit. Preferring cooler climates, they tolerate frost and even light snow. Identifying them correctly can be difficult.

▲ An unnamed sedum species Michele purchased from a local market. It is a fairly robust grower reaching 150 mm in height, here growing with its shallow roots around a dwarf red cordyline.

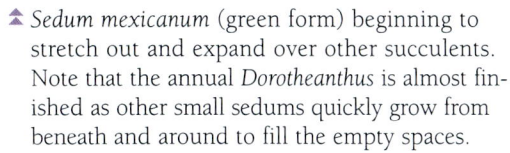

▲ *Sedum mexicanum* (green form) beginning to stretch out and expand over other succulents. Note that the annual *Dorotheanthus* is almost finished as other small sedums quickly grow from beneath and around to fill the empty spaces.

◥ Two different forms of *Sedum dasyphyllum*. The miniature form on the left has smooth leaves, with stems of approximately 5-7 mm in diameter.

▶▶ *Sedum rubrotinctum* 'Aurora'. Environmental stresses bring out the red colour in the leaves. Grow this plant hard to get the best colours. Do not pamper!

▶▶ *Sedum mexicanum* (gold form) showing compact winter growth, waiting for warm spring weather to triple its size in only four weeks.

◣ *Sedum nudum* becomes a miniature rich green carpet which is ideal for filling the spaces between larger sculptural plants.

▼ *Sedum lineare variegata*.

A NATURE STRIP 41

▲ A closeup of the green form of *Sedum mexicanum* beginning to flower. It flowers from tens of thousands of tiny buds (see picture bottom left which was taken two weeks later).

◀◀ *Sedum mexicanum* (green form) is one of the first sedums to flower in late spring when it produces a carpet of tiny yellow star-like flowers. During flowering it has expanded to be many times its original size, after which the exhausted plant, appearing to shrink, dies back to a smaller size.

◀ *In the background is Sedum mexicanum* exploding into flower. In the foreground is *Sedum nudum* which will soon begin to flower (see below).

▼ Four to six weeks later *Sedum nudum* begins to flower while behind it *Sedum mexicanum* (green form) dies back, with flowering finished. This picture is taken at a different angle from the photo on the left.

Sedums

The previous two pages looked at sedum foliage, growth habits and usage. These pages show the same plants only a month or two later (during late spring and early summer) when they are in full bloom. Gardeners growing sedums for their leaves and interesting growth forms often overlook their potential as flowering plants where they can rival many garden subjects in their performance.

▶▶ *Sedum dasyphyllum*, one of the tiniest sedums, is just coming into flower. The smaller stems seen rising up from the ground will soon flower too.

▼ The tiny blue *Sedum dasyphyllum* with a snow-like covering of flowers is still upstaged by the silver white of *Cotyledon orbiculata* 'Silver Waves'.

A NATURE STRIP 43

▲ *Aloe maculata* (formerly *A. saponaria*) and a close up of its flowers (picture below).
▼ Flowers through late spring and into summer.
◀◀ *Aloe 'spinosissima'*. This aloe regularly flowers in late winter, early spring in this garden. It is a dwarf aloe growing to an average height of about 400mm, before clumping into mounds.

Other succulents in flower

A number of very beautiful but less spectacular flowers are present during any season on the nature strip. This provides extra year round interest and colour.

▶▶ A close up of sempervivum flowers. These plants enjoy the cold of winter and with it comes the promise of flowers. The common idea that all succulents like the heat of summer is incorrect. Sempervivums are native to the European mountains where snow falls regularly.

◀ *Echeveria pulvinata*. Flowers and buds are almost the same colour as the leaves. These dramatic colours can only be obtained by growing the plant outdoors where frosty cold nights are followed by bright sunny days.

▼ *Echeveria 'Lucita'*, flowers. This echeveria is grown for its beautifully arranged leaves that are fringed with colour, not unlike a large flower in appearance.

The rest of the garden

Michele's pleasures in gardening are anything but stereotypical or succulent exclusive, so these few pictures were included to present an overall picture. A shaded tropical-look area fills the front garden. Palms, ferns, cycads and large leaved plants receive dappled shade from tall eucalypt and wattle trees.

▸ A favourite, though she has many, is *Justicia carnea*, a small to medium shrub that flowers for months. It was grown from a piece given to her by her mother, as were many of the first succulents used in the garden

▾ The backyard is where the 'forest' keeps out the suburban feel, as well as being home to many native birds and possums.

Care requirements

Although this nature strip garden needs little or no care to survive, Michele still prefers to tend it when she can. The more effort put in, the better it looks. After an extended overseas trip, it was a pleasant surprise to find that her succulents had fared better than the rest of the garden.

- Watering is not necessary but it can be helpful in the driest months or to establish small plants or seedlings.

- An arrangement of assorted sedum flowers in a vase is a colourful reward after tidying up this easy care garden.

- A light tidy up of old leaves and debris, as well as removal of weeds once or twice a year is recommended.

A NATURE STRIP

Further information on plants illustrated or grown in this garden

Plants	main attraction	flower colour	usage	shade tolerance	pot suitability
Aeonium 'Zwartkop' photo page 34	leaf colour flowers	yellow	sculpture background	low	excellent
Aloe maculata photo page 44	foliage flowers	orange	sculpture	low	moderate
Aloe 'spinosissima' photo page 44	flowers foliage	orange/red	sculpture background	low	yes
Cotyledon 'Silver Waves' photo page 43	leaf colour	orange	en masse background	low	moderate
Dorotheanthus bellidoniformis photo page 38	flowers	many	en masse	low	moderate
Echeveria 'Lucita' photo page 45	foliage	pink/orange	rosette	low	excellent
Echeveria pulidonis picture not included	flowers	yellow	en masse rosette	moderate	yes
Echeveria pulvinata photo page 45	leaf colour flowers	red and yellow	en masse	low	yes
Echeveria 'Violet Queen' photo page 34	leaf colour foliage	pink	en masse rosette	moderate	excellent
Graptoveria 'Huth's Pink' photo page 35	leaf colour symmetry	cream	en masse rosette	low	yes
Portulaca grandiflora photo page 39	flowers	many	en masse	low	moderate
Sedum dasyphyllum photo page 43	foliage flowers	white	en masse	moderate	moderate
Sedum lineare variegata photo page 41	foliage flowers	yellow	en masse	moderate	moderate
Sedum mexicanum (gold) photo page 41	foliage flowers	yellow	en masse	moderate	moderate
Sedum mexicanum (green) photo page 42	foliage flowers	yellow	en masse	moderate	moderate
Sedum nudum photo page 42	foliage flowers	white	en masse	moderate	moderate
Sedum rubrotinctum 'Aurora' photo page 41	foliage	yellow	en masse	low	moderate
Sedum species photo page 40	foliage flowers	yellow/white	en masse	moderate	moderate
Sempervivum species photo page 45	symmetry leaf colour	pink/white	en masse rosette	moderate	excellent
Senecio mandraliscae photo page 37	leaf colour	white	en masse background	moderate	not recommended

*Height and width are based on favorable garden situations and beginning with an 80mm size pot plant.

suitability for indoor situations	height & width after 1 year*	height & width after 5 years*	how does it spread?	usual method of propagation	additional information
sunny position	0.4 x 0.3 m	1 x 1 m	stems	cuttings	tolerates light frost
yes	0.1 x 0.2 m	0.2 x 0.4 m	offsets	offsets	frost hardy
not recommended	0.1 x 0.2 m	0.4 x 0.6 m	offsets	offsets	frost hardy
no	0.3 x 0.3 m	0.4 x 1 m	stems sprawling	cuttings	frost hardy prune to keep tidy
no	0.1 x 0.2 m	n/a	sprawling	seeds	winter/spring annuals many bright flowers
sunny position	0.1 x 0.2 m	0.2 x 0.2 m	solitary	head cuts	prune heads
not recommended	0.1 x 0.1 m	0.1 x 0.2 m	offsets	offsets	bright yellow flowers
sunny position	0.1 x 0.1 m	0.1 x 0.2 m	stems	cuttings	frost hardy
not recommended	0.1 x 0.2 m	0.1 x 0.2 m	offsets	offsets	frost hardy colourful in winter
not recommended	0.1 x 0.2 m	0.1 x 0.2 m	offsets	offsets	colourful in winter
no	0.1 x 0.2 m	n/a	sprawling	seeds	summer annuals
no	miniature	n/a	sprawling	leaves cuttings	excellent blue carpet
no	0.1 x 0.1 m	0.1 x 0.2 m	sprawling	leaves cuttings	prune to keep tidy
no	0.1 x 0.2 m	0.1 x 0.4 m	sprawling	leaves cuttings	prune to keep tidy frost hardy
no	0.1 x 0.2 m	0.1 x 0.4 m	sprawling	leaves cuttings	prune to keep tidy frost hardy
no	0.1 x 0.2 m	0.1 x 0.3 m	sprawling	leaves cuttings	prune to keep tidy frost hardy
no	0.1 x 0.2 m	0.1 x 0.3 m	sprawling	leaves cuttings	prune to keep tidy frost hardy
no	0.1 x 0.2 m	0.1 x 0.4 m	sprawling	leaves cuttings	prune to keep tidy frost hardy
no	0.1 x 0.1 m	0.1 x 0.2 m	offsets	offsets	frost hardy
no	0.2 x 0.2 m	0.3 x 0.3 m	sprawling	cuttings	prune to keep tidy tolerates light frost

50 A SEASIDE GARDEN

A Seaside Garden

Fiona and David have two acres of garden called 'Karkalla' by the ocean near a seaside town. Natural low growing and wind swept indigenous vegetation dominate much of the countryside here, including much of their garden. Fiona prefers the natural environment and promotes the use of indigenous plants in garden design. Near and around the immediate area of the house Fiona uses some exotic plants which she manages to blend into the indigenous environment as accent plants. Anything to be included has to look after itself as well as look good year round. Succulents, obtained via bits and pieces collected in the local area, proved easy and useful components in the garden scheme.

Strong, salt-laden and cold winds, with nutrient-poor sandy soil, restricted many other plant types that were tried, while the succulents thrived.

A view of the seaside which is only a short stroll from Fiona's property.

A statement of harmony by the front door. The shapes and colour of this *Cotyledon orbiculata* blend with the surrounding limestone wall of the house.

The entrance to the house tastefully uses sculptural plants to soften the lines of the house. In the foreground is a cluster of *Agave americana*. In the distance on the verandah itself, a large tub of aeoniums can be seen growing where little else could grow, let alone survive.

A SEASIDE GARDEN 51

Around the house

The natural vegetation near the house is blended with exotic plants, which are composed mostly of low-growing succulents that not only fit in well but also appear to thicken the immediate garden's vegetation. The garden makes extensive use of local granite gravel instead of lawn. The gravel supplies plant nutrients, lowers evaporation and suppresses weeds.

◂◂ Art in the garden, with Fiona looking on. Natural vegetation dominates much of the garden further away from the house. 'Koonya Beach Columns' by Chris Booth (N.Z sculptor)

▴ A Tiwi Pukamani pole from the Northern Territory
▾ Islands is on the far right. The green succulent with the yellow flowers is *Aeonium urbicum*. A lower growing *Cotyledon orbiculata* appears underneath. The picture at left was taken in summer while the picture at right was early the following spring.

52   A SEASIDE GARDEN

▲ *Aptenia cordifolia* beginning to carpet the granite gravel. This species, with its rich green foliage, is ideal for coastal areas and is a good alternative to a lawn.

▼ Without any lawn or watering of this garden, it is difficult to suggest that it looks dry when the plants look stunning and naturally healthy.

A SEASIDE GARDEN 53

Succulents in containers

Surviving only on irregular rain, succulents have been chosen for all the outdoor pottery for their resilience in harsh conditions. Because they maintain year round visual appeal they are used nearer the house and alongside pathways.

⬆ *Cotyledon orbiculata* with *Euphorbia characias* v. *wulfenii*.

⬇ This almost looks like a flower arrangement in a vase ready to go on the coffee table or to a floral art show. *Aeonium arboreum var. atropurpureum* growing out from between *Sedum praeltum*.

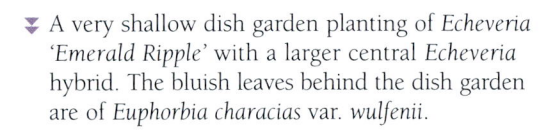

⬇ A very shallow dish garden planting of *Echeveria 'Emerald Ripple'* with a larger central *Echeveria* hybrid. The bluish leaves behind the dish garden are of *Euphorbia characias* var. *wulfenii*.

54 A SEASIDE GARDEN

▶▶ Colours and textures of all things visual are a consideration to Fiona. This crowded planting of *Crassula ovata* is well grown and yet stunted resulting in an intense reddish colour.

▼ A tastefully arranged side bench with seashells and potted echeverias.

An unwatered garden need not look dry and bare. Crowding the right plants together creates a fuller effect. *Cotyledon orbiculata* is in the foreground.

⏵⏵ A small stairway leading to the back of the house. Its right hand side drops away without a barrier. Contrasting *Aeonium 'Zwartkop'* and cotyledons were alternately planted alongside this edge to provide a warning for foot traffic.
Insert: As planted almost one year before.

⏷ Another pathway leading from the house into the garden is lined with tasteful potted succulents on the right while on the left succulents blend with exotic plants such as *Santolina*, *Convolvulus* and *Hebe* species.

A SEASIDE GARDEN 57

Further information on plants illustrated or grown in this garden

Plants	main attraction	flower colour	usage	shade tolerance	pot suitability
Aeonium arboreum not illustrated	foliage flowers	yellow	background	moderate	excellent
Aeonium atropurpureum photo page 54	foliage flowers	yellow	background sculpture	moderate	excellent
Aeonium urbicum photo page 52	shape	yellow	sculpture	moderate	low
Aeonium 'Zwartkop' photo page 57	foliage flowers	yellow	sculpture background	moderate	excellent
Agave americana photo page 50	shape	white	sculpture	moderate	excellent
Aptenia cordifolia photo page 53	leaf colour flowers	red or white	en masse	moderate	not recommended
Cotyledon orbiculata photo pages 51 & 54	leaf colour	orange	en masse background	low	moderate
Crassula ovata (dwarf) photo page 55	leaf colour shape	white	en masse borders	low	excellent
Echeveria 'Emerald Ripple' photo page 54	shape flowers	reddish	en masse borders	low	excellent
Echeveria hybrid photo page 54	shape flowers	reddish	sculpture	low	excellent
Sedum praeltum photo page 54	foliage flowers	yellow	background en masse	moderate	excellent

Other succulents which suit a seaside location (not pictured).

Plants	main attraction	flower colour	usage	shade tolerance	pot suitability
Aloe arborescens	flowers foliage	orange	background sculpture	moderate	not recommended
Beschorneria yuccoides	foliage flowers	pink	sculpture	moderate	not recommended
Carpobrotus species	flowers foliage	pink yellow	en masse background	low	no
Dudleya species	leaf colour shape	yellow	rosette	low	yes
Lampranthus species	flowers	many	en masse	low	no
Portulacaria afra	foliage shape	pink	background	moderate	yes
Puya species	foliage colour	many	background	moderate	not recommended
Senecio mandraliscae	foliage leaf colour	white	en masse background	moderate	not recommended

*Height and width are based on favorable garden situations and beginning with an 80mm size pot plant.

suitability for indoor situations	height & width after 1 year*	height & width after 5 years*	how does it spread?	usual method of propagation	additional information
sunny position	0.4 x 0.3 m	1 x 1 m	clumping	cuttings	prefers coastal conditions
sunny position	0.4 x 0.3 m	1 x 1 m	clumping	cuttings	prefers coastal conditions tolerates light frost
not recommended	0.1 x 0.3 m	0.3 x 1m	offsets	cuttings	prefers coastal conditions tolerates light frost
sunny position	0.4 x 0.3 m	1 x 1 m	clumping	cuttings	prefers coastal conditions tolerates light frost
not recommended	0.3 x 0.3 m	1.5 x 1.5 m	offsets	offsets •bulbils	hardy, fast growing frost hardy
no	0.1 x 0.8 m	0.1 x 2 m	sprawling	cuttings	very fast growing excellent ground cover
no	0.3 x 0.3 m	0.4 x 0.8 m	sprawling	cuttings	frost hardy prune to keep tidy
sunny position	0.2 x 0.1 m	0.3 x 0.2 m	solitary	cuttings	do not fertilize excellent bonsai subject
not recommended	0.1 x 0.1 m	0.3 x 0.3 m	offsets	offsets	tolerates light frost
not recommended	0.1 x 0.1 m	0.3 x 0.3 m	solitary	cuttings	tolerates light frost
sunny position	0.2 x 0.2 m	0.6 x 0.8 m	clumping	cuttings	frost hardy prune to keep tidy
not recommended	0.2 x 0.2 m	1 m x 1 m	stems	cuttings	attracts native birds frost hardy
no	0.2 x 0.2 m	0.7 x 1 m	mostly solitary	seeds	frost hardy
no	0.1 x 0.2 m	0.2 x 1.5 m	sprawling	cuttings	frost hardy
sunny position	0.1 x 0.1 m	0.2 x 0.1 m	mostly solitary	seeds	some varieties branch
no	0.1 x 0.10 m	0.2 x 1 m	clumping	cuttings	frost hardy prune to keep tidy
yes	0.2 x 0.2 m	1.2 x 1 m	stems	cuttings	frost hardy prune to shape
no	0.1 x 0.1 m	0.5 x 0.8 m	offsets	seeds offsets	frost hardy
no	0.2 x 0.2 m	0.3 x 1 m	sprawling	cuttings	prune to keep tidy tolerates light frosts

• Plantlets produced on flower stalks.

Country farmlet

Alexander has succulents growing across much of his five acre property; around the house, in a greenhouse, out in the field as well as around the farm dam in very useful ways.

Alexander has a long history with succulents going back twenty-five years. 'It all began with my wife surprising me with some plants which she had bought via mail order. I was overseas at the time and when I returned, I found twenty tin cans potted with these strange fat leaved plants. My first impressions were not favourable but as the cuttings developed and sent out new growth, I was intrigued by their colours, shapes and hardiness.'

He is equally interested in succulents and cactus, which are of course just a special subgroup of succulents. He was always interested in their survival strategies. This led to his initial visits to succulent habitats where he could see for himself where and how succulents survived.

⬆ After good rains, this lightly forested sheep and cattle country can be rich green and lush looking but regular dry hot summers and drought dominate.

◀◀ *Adenia glauca*. Caudiciforms (a group of stem
⬇ swelling succulents) like this one, are his favourites.
(insert) Flowers and new leaves.

60 COUNTRY FARMLET

▶▶ A range of echeverias which have been recently purchased through a mail order specialist. These are being tested for their suitability in the garden.

▼ Succulents may not be obvious at a glance, but in almost every corner and every pot, they are present. The right foreground was a rose garden but is currently being replaced with still more succulents. See the following pages.

Near the house

The garden hose can only reach so far. Even so, any plant used around or near the house has to have the ability to survive without watering. Alexander spends many months at a time overseas and has to leave the garden unattended. Succulents, while not the only plants that he grows, are by far the best performers.

▼ The most important thing of all in creating a successful succulent garden is good planning. Note the slightly raised garden beds which improve drainage.

◂◂ This former rose garden area is dissected by pathways creating four display beds, each with a different theme.

▼ This is more of a stone garden than anything else. Three large *Yucca rostrata* with a small notocactus planted in swirls.

This garden bed is geometric in design. In the foreground is *Senecio serpens* radiating out from the centre with a green *Crassula arborescens* var. *undulatifolia* used between each row. A raised bed in the centre begins with mondo grass with a central grouping of silver white *Cleistocactus strausii*.

Near the house

◂◂ Against the wall of a gazebo and entertainment area is this planter box of different jade plants. The outer two are *Portulacaria afra* (good luck Chinese jade), and the inner two are both forms of *Crassula ovata* (Chinese money trees). The association of good luck and good fortune in using these two plant types is no coincidence.

▼ Strawberry pot planted with three echeverias from left to right. *Echeveria agavoides*, *Echeveria 'Lucita'*, *Echeveria subsessilis*, with a green cascading branch of *Senecio petreae*.

▼ *Crassula arborescens* var. *undulatifolia* shown here flowering in early summer. It has a very compact growing habit.

▶▶ A disused seedling tray with bird wire drawn across it, was the framework for this newly made wall hanging.

◢ Four months later with absolutely no care given.

▼ Plenty of outdoor seating can be found dotted around the property, each one with a different garden view.

◢ *Senecio serpens* weaving its way around sandstone rocks. This scene can be viewed from the chairs pictured below.

COUNTRY FARMLET 65

In the field

A plantation of *Brachychiton rupestris*, a native Australian succulent (and a caudiciform). They can tolerate frosts as well as harsh dry conditions and will be shapely by themselves, increasing in beauty and value with age. They are generally dwarf compact trees without ever growing too tall or having branches that could break and fall. Brachychitons can be grown in large pots and tubs where they can easily be pruned into interesting shapes as with bonsai. *Brachychiton rupestris* also has a history of use by the indigenous people of central Queensland. The seeds, young roots and shoots are cooked and eaten. The wood contains a nutritious jelly. By making a hole in the trunk, a watery sap can be obtained for drinking.

⬆ Seasonal new growth is an attractive red.

⬇ Commercial plantation of *Brachychiton rupestris*. Each plant displays individual characteristics which are accentuated by pruning.

▶▶ Alexander pruning growing tips to make the trees grow bushier. Cockatoos and insects also do this naturally but haphazardly!

◢ As one reaches the far side of the property, the essential farm dam comes into view. A pathway leads onto the surroundiing embankment garden. Two *Brachychiton rupestris* greet you on either side of the entry path.

▼ A superb and ancient *Brachychiton rupestris* in habitat which has just dropped its leaves. This is uncommon for this plant as it mostly retains foliage throughout the year.

Farm dam

The dam was dug deep on gently sloping ground with one side banked over several metres high, with what was excavated. This was clay and poor subsoil which was then covered with a thin layer of loose gravely soil. Finding plants that would grow well and look good here was easy.

◂◂ In spring this view of the dam, full with rich green surrounds, can give a false impression. Most years, except for the succulents, it looks brown and dry with a very low water level.

▾ A glorious spring day with an abundance of water. Here a sandy gravel path leads around the dam perimeter. Wild ducks now frequent and nest here.

On this slope the clay bank is at its highest and most impoverished state. Note the native forest in the adjoining property, which is, during summer, an almost constant fire threat. The succulents on this slope provide an essential fire barrier.

Farm dam

In almost any month of the year one can find something in flower and here are just a few of the many highlights that make this garden area worthy of regular visits. While a dam is basically a water storage reserve, there is no reason why it cannot be a beautiful place as well.

Seating at a high point with a good view over much of the property as well as the dam below which looks more like an ornamental lake now, rather than just a farm dam. Light shade is provided by brachychitons.

This view leads away from the seats in the photo above. Hardy *Lampranthus* is in full bloom with larger aloe species behind.

This well-known and popular ponytail palm, *Nolina recurvata* is another stem swelling succulent also known as a caudiciform. People find its curious and interesting stem appealing for all sorts of reasons.

Chorisia speciosa. This medium size subtropical tree is very drought tolerant and does not mind being pruned into shape, making it very versatile. It is fast growing and flowers regularly in warmer weather (flower below is actual size). The canopy is a lush green. An interesting swollen trunk sometimes grows grotesque-looking thorns on the lower surface.

COUNTRY FARMLET 71

◀◀ *Agave parryi* inflorescence with plant (insert).
▲ Many agaves produce flower stalks which are several meters high. Above is a close up of *Agave parryi* flowers.

◀◀ *Ipomoea platense* has a large semi-submerged tuber which grows long vines each spring. Large flowers are produced throughout the summer.

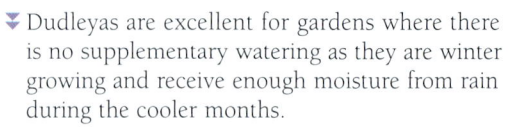

▼ Dudleyas are excellent for gardens where there is no supplementary watering as they are winter growing and receive enough moisture from rain during the cooler months.

Farm dam

▸▸ *Puya alpestris* This species has grass-like leaves and grows to approximately 1 meter high. The plant is not at all spectacular but its flowers are. The colour of the flowers are almost beyond photography's ability to capture.

◂ *Sedum praeltum* is very hardy and common in old run down gardens. It will grow anywhere as a low shrub, flowering in late winter and into spring. Bees love it.

▾ *Aloe cooperi*. This very interesting dwarf aloe species looks and grows like weedy grass until it flowers and then everybody seems to want a piece of it.

COUNTRY FARMLET 73

Uses of succulents

Many people have visited Alexander's property and have viewed his succulent gardens fleetingly. Few are aware that he also uses succulents as food plants. His understanding of what is edible comes mostly from observations made while travelling through rural villages while overseas.

◂◂ A prickly pear (*Opuntia robusta*). There are many different species of opuntia, all of which have edible fruit. This species is very productive with large apple-sized fruit. Interestingly, Alexander not only eats the fruit seasonally, but he also eats the cooked cactus. This is common in the southern USA and Mexico where you can also buy it in tin cans from the supermarket.

◂ (bottom) Here, fresh tender stems are being peeled and sliced to be cooked like green beans.

▾ Another cactus species with a large red, apple-sized fruit ready to pick. All cactus fruit are edible and many cactus species are used in Latin America for a whole range of things from the manufacture of soap, rope, and medicine, to alcohol.

◂ *Pereskia aculeata* 'Godseffiana'

▸ Alexander plucks the fresh growing tips and uses them in salads along with yucca flowers. He also cooks yucca flowers in omelettes.

◂ Yucca flowers have been used in the kitchen for thousands of years in Mexico. The very large and succulent petals of all yucca species, as well as the unopened buds, can be fried or eaten raw in salads.

▾ When *Aloe vera* is not available and is needed for burns and cuts, Alexander has a choice of other medicinal aloes to choose from. Two useful species are *Aloe ferox* and *Aloe africana* (pictured below).

COUNTRY FARMLET 75

Further information on plants illustrated or grown in this garden

Plants	main attraction	flower colour	usage	shade tolerance	pot suitability
Adenia glauca photo page 60	caudex (stem)	yellow	climbing vine sculpture	moderate	yes
Agave parryi photo page 72	symmetry	seldom flowers	sculpture	low	yes
Aloe africana photo page 75	shape flowers	orange	sculpture	low	moderate
Brachychiton rupestris photo page 66	shape thick trunk	reddish	sculpture shade tree	low	yes
Chorisia speciosa photo page 71	stem flowers	red	sculpture shade tree	low	not recommended
Crassula ovata photo page 63	leaf colour stem	white	sculpture background	low	excellent
Echeveria agavoides photo page 64	symmetry leaf colour	red/yellow	rosette en masse	low	excellent
Echeveria subsessilis photo page 64	leaf colour symmetry	pink	rosette en masse	low	excellent
Ipomoea platense photo page 72	flowers caudex (root)	purple	climbing vine background	low	yes
Lampranthus sp. photo page 70	flowers	purple	en masse	low	not recommended
Nolina recurvata photo page 71	shape stem	white	sculpture en masse	high	yes
Notocactus sp photo page 62	flowers	yellow	sculpture flowers	low	excellent
Opuntia robusta photo page 74	shape colourful fruit	yellow	sculpture	low	yes
Pereskia 'Godseffiana' photo page 75	leaf colour	pink	background	moderate	yes
Portulacaria afra photo page 64	leaf colour shape	pink	sculpture en masse	low	yes
Puya alpestris photo page 73	flowers	blue	sculpture	low	not recommended
Sedum praeltum photo page 73	foliage flowers	yellow	background en masse	moderate	moderate
Kleinia petreae photo page 64	foliage flowers	yellow	cascades en masse	moderate	no
Senecio serpens photo page 63	leaf colour	white	en masse borders	low	no
Yucca rostrata photo page 62	leaf colour symmetry	white	sculpture	low	moderate

*Height and width are based on favorable garden situations and beginning with an 80mm size pot plant.

suitability for indoor situations	height & width after 1 year*	height & width after 5 years*	how does it spread?	usual method of propagation	additional information
sunny position	0.4 x 0.1 m	1.2 x 0.2 m	vine	seeds cuttings	winter deciduous cannot tolerate frost
not recommended	0.1 x 0.1 m	0.3 x 0.3 m	offsets	offsets seeds	frost hardy best planted in threes
sunny position	0.2 x 0.2 m	1 x 1 m	solitary	seeds	moderately frost hardy
no	0.3 x 0.1 m	1.5 x 0.2 m	solitary	seeds	grows huge with time frost hardy
no	0.5 x 0.1 m	1.5 x 0.2 m	solitary	seeds	tolerates light frost large tree
sunny position	0.3 x 0.2 m	1 x 0.6 m	solitary	cuttings leaves	tolerates light frost excellent for bonsai
sunny position	0.2 x 0.2 m	0.3 x 0.3 m	offsets	offsets	frost tolerant very hardy
sunny position	0.2 x 0.2 m	0.3 x 0.3 m	offsets	offsets leaves	frost tolerant
sunny position	0.5 x 0.5 m	2 x 0.5 m	vine	seeds	winter deciduous frost hardy
no	0.2 x 0.4 m	0.4 x 1 m	creeping or clumping	cuttings	frost hardy
yes	0.3 x 0.2 m	1 x 0.7 m	solitary	seeds	tolerates light frost
not recommended	0.1 x 0.1 m	0.2 x 0.2 m	solitary	seeds	frost hardy very hardy
not recommended	0.2 x 0.2 m	1 x 1 m	stems	cuttings	very frost hardy illegal in some areas
yes	0.2 x 0.2 m	0.5 x 1 m	sprawling edible leaves	cuttings	protect from frost
sunny position	0.2 x 0.3 m	1 x 1 m	sprawling	cuttings	tolerates light frost prune for shape
no	0.3 x 0.3 m	0.8 x 0.8 m	offsets	seeds offsets	frost hardy
sunny position	0.2 x 0.2 m	0.6 x 0.8 m	sprawling	cuttings	frost hardy prune to keep tidy
sunny position	0.3 x 0.2 m	1 x 0.6 m	sprawling	cuttings	tolerates light frost
not recommended	0.1 x 0.2 m	0.2 x 0.5 m	rhizomes	cuttings	frost hardy compact growth
not recommended	0.2 x 0.2 m	1.2 x 1 m	solitary	seeds	frost hardy spectacular flowers

A hillside country garden

William Martin's 'Wigandia' is a three acre garden established on a hill of volcanic scoria. With strong winds and minimal access to water, this would have seemed a daunting task to many. Using imagination and local knowledge, William has achieved what others wouldn't even dare to try. He pieced together his own special masterpiece. This garden, which is interesting and pleasing to the eye, as well as challenging, is low in maintenance. Much admired and featured in numerous publications, it has been given one of the highest complements: 'I have seen the future of gardening and it is called Wigandia!' (Leo Schofield).

▶▶ Mid spring view from William's garden of the mostly bare surrounding hills. Winds and summer heat turn everything but his garden into a barren-looking landscape.

▼▼ The view looking in the opposite direction to the photo on the right. William's garden has been called 'a garden of the sun' because it is very exposed to the sun and weather, with little overhead canopy to provide shade.

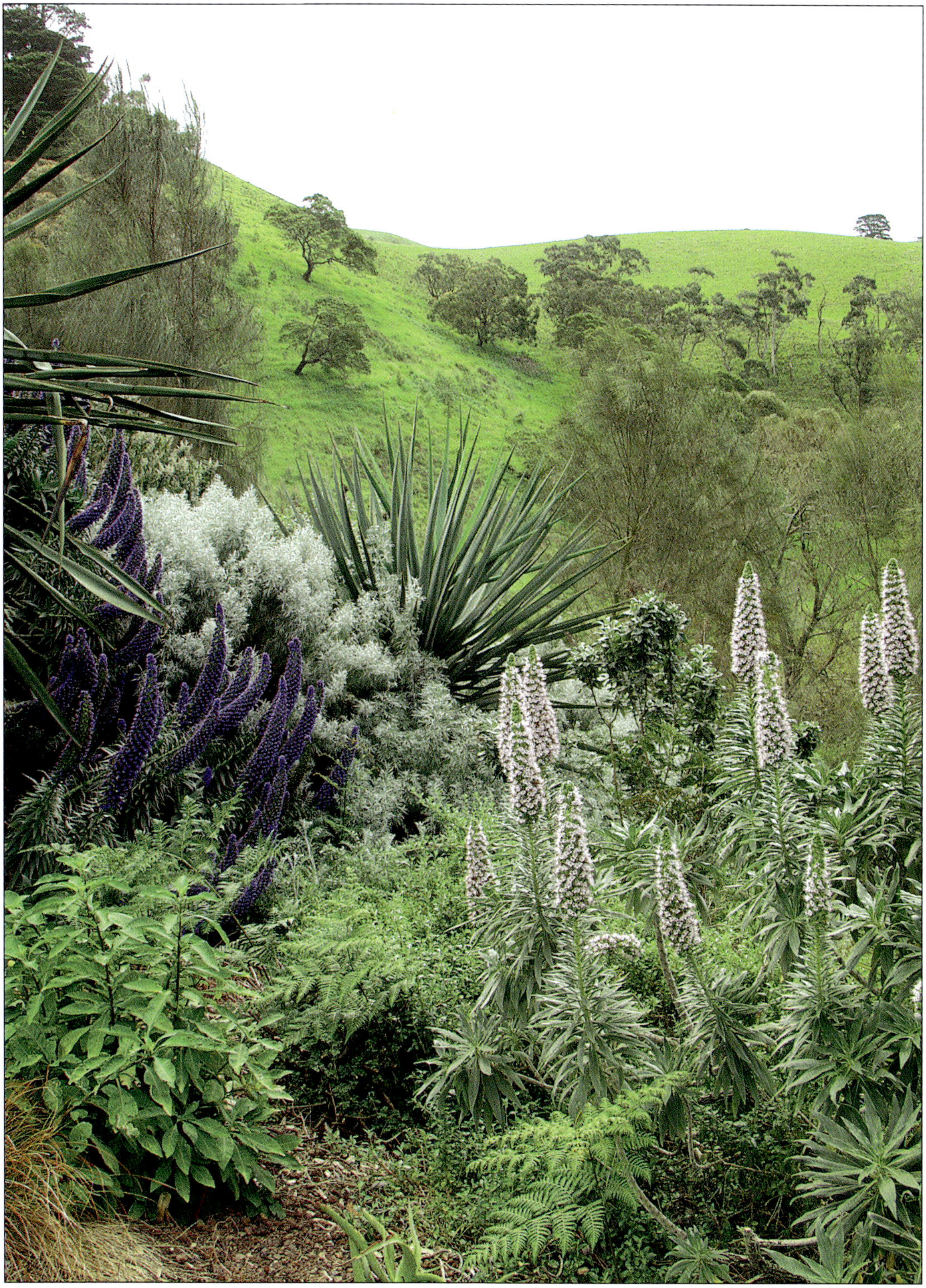

The entrance

The first casual impression as you enter William's garden is one of disorientation. There are no sweeping lawns or avenues of trees. In fact, little if anything of what one would expect of a great garden. Besides obscure art, among other things, using recycled metal, the first grand vista is of a dry gravel covered open space with low crowded shrubs around its perimeter. Then the magic begins. Pathways meander in every direction. The fullness and luxuriance of the garden only then becomes apparent. Within his garden William has used plants both practically and artistically. His artistic abilities are not restricted to plant usage, as can be seen on these pages.

◂◂ Looking up towards the house along the main entrance and driveway.

◂ Every month of the year there is something in flower. Here blue agapanthus takes the stage, as low growing *Echeveria glauca* var. *pumila* finishes its show of bell-like flowers as seen in the foreground.

◂ It is true to say the pathways are dry and bare looking, but the garden beds they adjoin are rich and full of colour. Foliage not flowers are the key here. (sculpture by Jon Dixon)

◂ William (seen standing on the left) enjoys giving garden advice. He has had over one thousand people visit his much publicised and talked about garden in a single day.

▾ Mid summer, and looking full and green. This is achieved with only sparse rainfall to rely on, adding to the uniqueness of this garden. Succulents featured here are *Yucca recurvifolia* (flowering) along with *Echeveria glauca* var. *pumila*, which is growing at the edge of the pathway.

▾ The large open space of scoria instead of lawn is deceiving in its bare dry look when the garden beds that surround it are the exact opposite. In the foreground is *Sedum 'Vera Jamieson'* in flower.

HILLSIDE COUNTRY GARDEN 81

Spring in the garden

Plant selection and usage as an art form is William's forte. Foliage colour, shape, form and texture all play a part in this artist's palette. Visitors are quickly drawn to a myriad of plant types and combinations that are not restricted by formal edges or boundaries and seem to flow naturally into the pathways.

They say nice sunny spring days bring out the crowds. This must have been one of those days. The echiums in the far right of picture below and the picture on the right also attracted a lot of attention from dozens of butterflies.

▶▶ Dramatic foliage combinations such as this are always a crowd pleaser. A red cordyline in the foreground with the larger silver leafed artichoke in the back.

◀ Succulents as art and sculpture. *Cotyledon macrantha* coming into flower with *Agave angustifolia* in the centre, with a large *Furcraea* species as a backdrop.

▼ Whether in a pot or not, it seems to look right. Blue *Senecio mandraliscae* and silver white *Cotyledon orbiculata* behind a potted *Yucca rigida*.

HILLSIDE COUNTRY GARDEN

Garden art

Art in this garden is unrestricted by rules or boundaries, and so is very much open to interpretation. What is unquestionably clear is that a talented artist has been at work here, using diverse and dramatic foliage plants as a base.

◀◀ A bare tree stump radiates its arms in front of a massive *Phormium* species (New Zealand flax). At its base is a flowering *Sedum 'Vera Jamieson'*.

▼ Placement of art, as with placement of each plant species is never a haphazard event. *Senecio mandraliscae* in the foreground.
(sculpture by Jon Dixon)

▸ The more you look at the rock walls, the more of interest is found. Here, dry grass and *Echeveria glauca* var. *pumila* provide an unusual combination.

▼ William's son Rory alongside a scene of practical art. The seating and the immediate surrounds of *Echeveria glauca* var. *pumila* planted beneath, work together for effect.

Succulents in the garden

William likes most plants but uses only those that are practical in his scheme of gardening. Plants with very low maintenance requirements and a strong year round visual appeal are especially desirable. To enjoy the most with the least effort, succulents, grasses and strappy leaved plants have been more widely used. Through experimentation over the years those plants which might have seemed desirable but have not performed well have been rejected. As you might expect, succulents have proved to be able to handle the harsh conditions, and their usage, with and around other plants, has now come to prominence in this garden.

◀◀ *Cotyledon macrantha* coming into flower with two small plants of *Senecio mandraliscae* in the foreground. Part of an *Aloe arborescens* can just be seen on the far right.

◀ Pinks and blues go well together in a tapestry with green. *Graptoveria* 'Huth's Pink' in the foreground with blue *Senecio mandraliscae* behind.

◀ There is nothing bare or dry looking about this picture. *Echeveria imbricata* looking very much like a flower.

▶▶ The stage was already set and complete and then a tulip came into the picture.

◀ A blend of leaf shapes and colours. The bergenia to the left need not flower to be effective, but the flowers are an added bonus for a few weeks each year.

▼ This stunning specimen of *Aloe maculata* (formerly *Aloe saponaria*) boldly contrasting with the mostly green foliage around it.

HILLSIDE COUNTRY GARDEN 87

On the steep hillsides

Whereas some of William's garden is on level or gently sloping land, much of it is steep, requiring extra skill in the planning. Steps, retaining walls and embankments are positioned with suitable pathways to match.

◂◂ *Aeonium arboreum* 'Zwartkop' is being used to mark the edge of the pathway.

▾ The steep slope is softened with good plant placement. Silver white *Cotyledon orbiculata* is planted in masses to the left of the path, with blue *Senecio mandraliscae* clumps on the right. The yellow flowers in the distance are of *Sedum praeltum*.

▶▶ A large mass planting of *Cotyledon orbiculata* flowering in summer while the nearby hillsides appear dry and bare. Succulents are excellent for erosion control on hillsides such as this.

◀◀ A native she oak has dropped leaves all over this recently planted site. Bracken fern was threatening in the background and so plastic weed matting was used and then pierce planted, before being covered with gravel. Within three months it will be a carpet of *Aeonium domesticum*.

▼ This retaining wall becomes a garden in itself. *Echeveria glauca* var. *pumila* growing exactly as echeverias do in nature, along mountain cliffs.

HILLSIDE COUNTRY GARDEN 89

Further information on plants illustrated or grown in this garden

Plants	main attraction	flower colour	usage	shade tolerance	pot suitability
Aeonium domesticum photo page 89	shape	white	en masse background	moderate	excellent
Aeonium tabuliforme (not pictured)	symmetry leaf colour	white	rosette en masse	high	yes
Aeonium 'Zwartkop' photo page 88	foliage flowers	yellow	sculpture background	low	excellent
Agave angustifolia photo page 83	symmetry shape	yellow	sculpture	low	moderate
Aloe arborescens photo page 87	shape flowers	red	sculpture background	low	moderate
Aloe aristata (not pictured)	shape	reddish	rosette en masse	moderate	yes
Aloe maculata photo page 87	foliage flowers	orange	sculpture	low	moderate
Cotyledon orbiculata photo page 88	leaf colour	orange	en masse background	low	excellent
Cotyledon macrantha photo page 83	leaf colour shape	orange	en masse background	moderate	yes
Echeveria imbricata photo page 86	symmetry leaf colour	pink/ orange	rosette en masse	moderate	excellent
Echeveria glauca v pumila photo page 85	symmetry	pink/ yellow	rosette en masse	moderate	yes
Euphorbia caput-medusae (not pictured)	shape	yellow	sculpture	low	yes
Furcraea species photo page 83	shape	white	sculpture	low	not recommended
Graptoveria 'Huth's Pink' photo page 86	leaf colour symmetry	cream	rosette en masse	low	yes
Sedum praeltum photo page 88	foliage	yellow	background en masse	moderate	moderate
Sedum 'Vera Jamieson' photo page 84	foliage	pink	flowers background	low	moderate
Senecio mandraliscae photo page 84	leaf colour	white	en masse background	moderate	moderate
Yucca recurvifolia photo page 81	foliage flowers	cream	sculpture flowers	moderate	moderate
Yucca rigida photo page 83	foliage flowers	cream	sculpture flowers	moderate	moderate
Puya species (not pictured)	shape leaf colour	varies	sculpture background	moderate	not recommended

suitability for indoor situations	height & width after 1 year*	height & width after 5 years*	how does it spread?	usual method of propagation	additional information
sunny position	0.3 x 0.3 m	0.4 x 0.5 m	stems	cuttings	frost hardy
yes	0.1 x 0.2 m	0.1 x 0.4 m	solitary	seeds leaves	tolerates light frost prefers shade
sunny position	0.4 x 0.3 m	1 x 1 m	stems	cuttings	tolerates light frosts
not recommended	0.3 x 0.3 m	0.8 x 1 m	offsets •bulbils	offsets •bulbils	remove untidy offsets frost hardy
sunny position	0.3 x 0.2 m	1 x 0.6 m	stems	cuttings	frost hardy
yes	0.1 x 0.1 m	0.2 x 0.3 m	offsets	offsets	frost hardy prefers some shade
yes	0.1 x 0.2 m	0.2 x 0.4 m	offsets	offsets	frost hardy
no	0.3 x 0.3 m	0.4 x 1 m	sprawling	cuttings	prune to keep tidy frost hardy
no	0.3 x 0.2 m	0.5 x 0.8 m	sprawling	cuttings	prune to keep tidy tolerates light frosts
sunny position	0.1 x 0.2 m	0.2 x 0.5 m	offsets	offsets	frost hardy
sunny position	0.1 x 0.2 m	0.1 x 0.4 m	offsets	offsets	frost hardy
not recommended	0.1 x 0.2 m	0.2 x 0.8 m	solitary	seeds	frost hardy
no	0.3 x 0.3 m	1.5 x 1.5 m	solitary	•bulbils	fast growing tolerates light frosts
not recommended	0.1 x 0.2 m	0.1 x 0.3 m	offsets	offsets	frost hardy, best colours in cooler months
sunny position	0.2 x 0.2 m	0.6 x 0.8 m	sprawling	cuttings	frost hardy prune to keep tidy
no	0.3 x 0.2 m	0.3 x 0.4 m	clumping	division	winter deciduous tolerates frosts
no	0.3 x 0.3 m	0.3 x 1 m	sprawling	cuttings	prune to keep tidy tolerates light frost
no	0.2 x 0.2 m	0.8 x 0.8 m	offsets	offsets	frost hardy edible flowers
no	0.2 x 0.2 m	0.8 x 0.8 m	solitary	seeds	frost hardy edible flowers
no	0.3 x 0.3 m	1 x 1 m	offsets	seeds offsets	frost hardy

*...ight and width are based on favorable garden situations and beginning with an 80mm size pot plant.
*...ntlets produced on flower stalks.

A cactus garden

Jim and his family operate a vegetable farm on a large country property. Whenever Jim has spare time he heads out to his desert garden of cactus and other succulents. However, having to work the vegetable business very intensively on a seasonal basis cuts severely into recreational time in the garden. What first began as an interest in cactus, passed down from his father has seen Jim transform the vacant land near the house into a desert scene. Cactus are his main pleasure, proving themselves time and again to be perfect garden subjects for him as they can go without care for months on end. The perfect plants for a busy farmer. Recent years have seen Jim expand the area of the garden to cover several acres.

▲ Close to the house are lawns and shady trees. Only a short stroll behind the house a path leads to the open and very sunny cactus garden.

▼ Jim is a tall man at over 2 meters and yet he appears dwarfed alongside this big *Ferocactus horridus*. This fruit laden specimen is over forty years old.

▼ Other succulents, such as this flowering aloe, are also present to a lesser degree in parts of the garden.

▲ Paths lead throughout the cactus garden. Each area is planted with related species and reflects the regions of their native habitat. This part of the South American section contains mostly oreocereus and espostoas.

CACTUS COUNTRY 93

Cactus on a grand scale

While many cactus can be kept small and contained happily in pots for years, there are just as many that have the potential to reach grand proportions if given ideal conditions. With dry, hot and very sunny summers as well as frosty winters, Jim has found that cactus grow best for him when they are planted in the garden where their roots can grow unrestricted. This cactus garden is large by anyone's standards and gives Jim the freedom to grow plants big.

A great assortment of succulent types are grown in the garden. From these pictures, it is clear that cactus, which are Jim's favourites, have performed very well in this garden situation. Once established in the sandy soil of an ancient riverbed, large growing varieties can gain up to 400 mm or more in height in a single summer.

▲ *Cereus peruvianus*, here growing large enough to cast shade onto the pathway and seats beneath the arching branches.

▼ There is always something to see and enjoy. If not the plants themselves, then the flowers and the birds and butterflies which they attract. More bird species nest in these cactus than in all the trees on neighbouring properties.

▶▶ To see a forest of mostly South American cactus like this outside of their native habitat is quite surprising. In the foreground and midground are different trichocereus. The white hairy plants are oreocereus and espostoas.

◢ Three young *Agave americana* plants in front of a flowering *Ferocactus acanthoides*. Behind is a larger *Ferocactus horridus* and slightly to the right is a *Carnegia gigantea*. Framing this picture are two *Yucca aloifolia*.

▼ *Echinocereus stramineus* in the foreground. Behind is a large opuntia.

CACTUS COUNTRY   95

This could be a natural scene from the high, dry Andes in South America. The mature candelabra-like specimen in the foreground is *Espostoa lanata*. Behind is the very golden *Weberocereus johnstonii*. Knowing their size and growth habits in nature has helped Jim space them appropriately in this garden.

▶▶ *Oreocereus celcianus*. The 'old man of the Andes' is more dwarf and shrub-like than many of its taller relatives. Its stems can reach 150 mm in diameter.

◀ Part of the Mexican section of the garden. In the front is *Myrtillocactus geometrizans* and directly behind and growing above it is *Polaskia chichipe* which is looking particularly robust and vigorous.

▼ *Echinocactus grusonii*, the golden barrel, is found in the Mexican section of the garden. Every cactus garden should have at least one of these much prized plants.

Cactus flowers

Cactus have had a reputation which suggests that they do not flower very often or that you have to wait seven years for them to flower again. In Jim's garden they out perform most other garden plants and of the thousands of cactus that are grown here, most flower annually. Mid to late spring is the best time for flowering, but any month of the year can find flowers either coming or going. Most of these pictures were taken on a single visit in summer. On still nights the sweet perfume from some varieties can travel many kilometers.

Trichocereus species

Notocactus uebelmannianus

Notocactus herteri

Trichocereus schickendantzii

▲ *Notocactus magnificus*

▶▶ *Trichocereus* hybrid

◀ *Echinocereus blankii* var. *leonensis*

▼ *Trichocereus grandiflorus*

Some challenges

With such a perfect environment for cactus, what can go wrong? It is interesting to see some of the obstacles and challenges with which Jim is sometimes faced. No garden is without obstacles: be it a rose garden or a bed of marigolds, and yet here there are very few problems in comparison. Requiring almost no attention for pests and diseases or watering, Jim likes the cactus looking natural and the bigger the better. Handling these giants, moving them or cutting them back is a skill learnt from experience.

◀◀ Jim inspects the growth of his favourite cactus, a young specimen of *Trichocereus pasacana*. This species grows to over 10 metres in height.

▼ When this *Agave americana* grew too large and over the path, the spiny leaf tips were cut off. Gazanias were also planted under its spread to keep visitors out of harms way.

▲ A large multi-branched *Trichocereus bridgesii* had
◤ become top-heavy and fell over in the wind. This form of the species was too spiky and awkward to be propped up again. All the long branches were cut off and laid alongside the main stump. After a matter of months with all parts lying in the sun, new growth has come forth, not only from the old stump, but from the cut off branches as well. These branches can be planted elsewhere to start again, or left to make a big forest.

▶▶ *Ferocactus horridus*. This plant grew two new branches on one side, displacing the centre of gravity, and pulling the main body over. This is the same plant seen on page 92. Jim's next big challenge will be to return it to an upright position.

Further information on plants illustrated or grown in this garden

Plants	main attraction	flower colour	usage	shade tolerance	pot suitability
Agave americana photo page 100	shape	white	sculpture	moderate	excellent
Carnegia gigantea photo page 95	shape	white	sculpture	low, full sun is best	yes
Cereus peruvianus photo page 94	shape, flowers	white	background	low, full sun is best	yes
Echinocereus stramineus photo page 95	flowers	varies	sculpture, en masse	low, full sun is best	excellent
Espostoa species photo page 96	shape, white wool	white	background	low, full sun is best	yes
Ferocactus acanthoides photo page 95	shape	reddish	sculpture	low, full sun is best	yes
Ferocactus horridus photo page 92	shape	reddish	sculpture	low, full sun is best	yes
Myrtillocactus geometrizans photo page 97	shape	white	background, sculpture	low, full sun is best	yes
Notocactus herteri photo page 98	flowers	peach	sculpture, borders	low, full sun is best	yes
Notocactus magnificus photo page 99	shape, flowers	yellow	sculpture	low, full sun is best	yes
Notocactus uebelmannianus photo page 98	flowers	purple	sculpture, borders	low, full sun is best	yes
Opuntia species photo page 95	shape, flowers	varies	background	low, full sun is best	yes
Oreocereus celcianus photo page 97	shape	pink	sculpture, background	low, full sun is best	yes
Polaskia chichipe photo page 97	shape	white	background, sculpture	low, full sun is best	yes
Trichocereus bridgesii photo page 101	shape	white	background	low, full sun is best	yes
Trichocereus grandiflora photo page 99	flowers	red	sculpture, borders	low, full sun is best	yes
Trichocereus pasacana photo page 100	shape	white	sculpture	low, full sun is best	yes
Trichocereus schickendantzii photo page 98	shape	white	sculpture	low, full sun is best	yes
Weberocereus johnstonii photo page 96	shape	white	sculpture	low, full sun is best	yes
Yucca aloifolia photo page 95	shape	white	sculpture	moderate	not recommended

*Height and width are based on favorable garden situations and beginning with an 80mm size pot plant.

suitability for indoor situations	height & width after 1 year*	height & width after 5 years*	how does it spread?	usual method of propagation	additional information
not recommended	0.3 x 0.3 m	1.5 x 1.5 m	offsets	offsets •bulbils	hardy, fast growing frost hardy
not recommended	0.1 x 0.1 m	0.3 x 0.1 m	solitary	seed	very slow growing requires hot summers
not recommended	0.3 x 0.1 m	1.5 x 0.2 m	branches	cuttings	hardy, fast growing large showy flowers
not recommended	0.2 x 0.2 m	0.3 x 0.4 m	clumping	cuttings	frost hardy
sunny position	0.1 x 0.1 m	0.4 x 0.1 m	branches	seed	white wool looks best in low rainfall areas
not recommended	0.1 x 0.1 m	0.8 x 0.3 m	mostly solitary	seed	requires hot summers
not recommended	0.1 x 0.1 m	0.3 x 0.3 m	mostly solitary	seed	requires hot summers
not recommended	0.1 x 0.1 m	1 x 0.8 m	branches	cuttings seeds	requires hot summers
sunny position	0.1 x 0.1 m	0.2 x 0.2 m	solitary	seed	tolerates cool climates
sunny position	0.1 x 0.1 m	0.2 x 0.3 m	clumping	offsets	tolerates cool climates
sunny position	0.1 x 0.1 m	0.2 x 0.2 m	solitary	seed	tolerates cool climates
not recommended	0.2 x 0.2 m	1 x 1 m	clumping	cuttings	many species prohibited in Q, NSW, SA
not recommended	0.2 x 0.1 m	1 x 0.2 m	branches	seed	tolerates cool climates
not recommended	0.2 x 0.1 m	1 x 0.6 m	branches	cuttings	requires summer heat
not recommended	0.2 x 0.1 m	1 x 0.6 m	clumping	cuttings	requires hot summers
sunny position	0.2 x 0.1 m	0.4 x 0.3 m	clumping	cuttings	tolerates cool climates flowers when young
not recommended	0.1 x 0.1 m	0.5 x 0.2 m	mostly solitary	seed	tolerates cool climates
not recommended	0.1 x 0.1 m	0.5 x 0.2 m	clumping	seed	requires hot summers
not recommended	0.1 x 0.1 m	1.2 x 0.2 m	branches	seed	requires hot summers
not recommended	0.3 x 0.2 m	1.5 x 0.6 m	offsets	offsets	hardy, fast growing tolerates light frosts

• Plantlets produced on flower stalks.

Index

Adenia glauca 60, 76
Aeonium 'Zwartkop' 34, 48, 57, 58, 88, 90
Aeonium arboreum 58
Aeonium arboreum var. *atropurpureum* 54
Aeonium atropurpureum 58
Aeonium domesticum 89, 90
Aeonium tabuliforme 90
Aeonium urbicum 52, 58
Agave americana 13, 51, 58, 95, 100, 102
Agave angustifolia 83, 90
Agave angustifolia variegata 13
Agave bracteosa 19
Agave harvardiana 20
Agave parryi 72, 76
Aloe saponaria 44
Aloe africana 75, 76
Aloe arborescens 58, 87, 90
Aloe aristata 13, 90
Aloe cooperi 73
Aloe khamiesensis 18
Aloe maculata 44, 48, 87, 90
Aloe pillansii, 17
Aloe plicatilis 30
Aloe saponaria 87
Aloe 'spinosissima' 44, 48
Annanus comosum variegatum 13
Aptenia cordifolia 53, 58
Beschorneria yuccoides 58
Brachychiton rupestris 66, 67, 76
Carnegia gigantea 95, 102
Carpobrotus 58
Cereus peruvianus 94, 102
'chinese money trees' 64
Chorisia speciosa 70, 71, 76
Cleistocactus straussii 63
convolvulus 57
cordyline 40
Cotyledon macrantha 83, 87, 90
Cotyledon orbiculata 51, 52, 54, 56, 58, 83, 88, 89, 90
Cotyledon orbiculata 'Silver Waves' 43, 48
Crassula arborescens var. *undulatifolia* 64
Crassula ovata 55, 58, 63, 64, 76
Dorotheanthus bellidoniformis 38, 39, ,41 48
Dudleya 58, 72
Echeveria 'Afterglow' 25, 30

Echeveria agavoides 64, 76
Echeveria 'Arlie Wright' 27, 30
Echeveria 'Big Red' 27, 30
Echeveria 'Bittersweet' 26, 30
Echeveria 'Blue Curl' 27, 30
Echeveria derenbergii 30
Echeveria 'Doris Taylor' 30
Echeveria elegans 27, 30
Echeveria 'Emerald Ripple' 54, 58
Echeveria 'Fasciculata' 26, 30
Echeveria 'Fireball' 25
Echeveria glauca var. *pumila* 81, 85, 89, 90
Echeveria hybrid 58
Echeveria imbricata 87, 90
Echeveria lilacina 25, 30
Echeveria 'Lucita' 45, 48, 64
Echeveria 'Mauna Loa' 27, 30
Echeveria multicaulis 26
Echeveria pallida 27, 30
Echeveria pulidonis 48
Echeveria pulvinata 45, 48
Echeveria 'Red Edge' 27, 30
Echeveria 'Rococo' 25, 30
Echeveria species 19
Echeveria subsessilis 64, 76
Echeveria 'Topsy Turvy' 27, 30
Echeveria 'Violet Queen' 29, 30, 34, 48
Echinocereus blankii var. *leonensis* 99
Echinocereus stramineus 95
Espostoa lanata 96
Espostoa species 93, 102
Euphorbia caput-medusae 90
Euphorbia caracias v. *wulfenii* 54
Euphorbia lactea 13
Euphorbia milii 21
Ferocactus acanthoides 95, 102
Ferocactus horridus 92, 95, 101, 102
Furcraea species 83, 90
Graptopetalum paraguayense 24, 30
Graptoveria 'Huth's Pink' 28, 34, 48, 87, 90
Hebe 57
hyacinths 37
Ipomoea platense 72, 76
jonquils 37
Justicia carnea 46
Kleinia petreae 76
Lampranthus 58, 70, 76
lithops 7
Livingstone daisies 38
Myrtillocactus geometrizans 97, 102

Nolina recurvata 71, 76
Notocactus 62, 76
Notocactus herteri 98, 102
Notocactus magnificus 99, 102
Notocactus uebelmannianus 98, 102
Opuntia robusta 74, 76
Opuntia species 102
oreocereus 93
Oreocereus celcianus 97, 102
Pereskia aculeata 'Godseffiana' 75, 76
Phormium species 84
Polaskia chichipe 97, 102
Portulaca grandiflora 38, 48
Portulacaria afra 58, 64, 76
Puya 58
Puya alpestris 73, 76
Puya raimondii 18
Puya species 90
Santolina 57
Sedum dasyphyllum 41, 43, 48
Sedum lineare variegata 41, 48
Sedum mexicanum 37, 41, 42, 48
Sedum morganianum 11
Sedum nudum 41, 42, 48
Sedum nussbaumerianum 24, 30
Sedum praeltum 54, 58, 73, 76, 88, 90
Sedum rubrotinctum 'Aurora' 41, 48
Sedum species 48
Sedum 'Vera Jamieson' 81, 90
sedums 40, 43
Sempervivum tectorum 30
sempervivums 13, 45, 48
Senecio mandraliscae 48, 58, 83, 84, 87, 88, 90
Senecio serpens 63, 65, 76
Trichocereus bridgesii 101, 102
Trichocereus grandiflora 99, 102
Trichocereus hybrid 99
Trichocereus pasacana 21, 100, 102
Trichocereus schickendantzii 98, 102
Trichocereus species 98
trichocereus 95
Triteleia sp. 37
Weberocereus johnstonii 96, 102
Welwitchia mirabilis 17
yucca 75
Yucca aloifolia 13, 95, 102
Yucca recurvifolia 81, 90
Yucca rigida 83, 90
Yucca rostrata 62, 76